Orton Gillingham Decodable Readers

Unlock Reading Success with Decodable Texts and Phonics-Based Passages for Early and Struggling Readers and Students with Dyslexia

By Kate Mendoza

Table of contents

Page	Title	Target Skill
6	🎁 Your free gift 🎁	-
7	Introduction	-
11	Dan's fat cat	CVC, Short a sound
12	Liz and her big pig	CVC, Short i sound
13	Ben and Meg	CVC, Short e sound
14	Jon's dog	CVC, Short o sound
15	My pup	CVC, Short u sound
16	Ann likes ants	Short vowels: initial position
17	Pam's cat	CVC, Short vowels sound
18	The red hen	CVC, Short vowels sound
19	My pig	CVC, Short vowels sound
20	Nat and his pup	CVC, Short vowels sound

Page	Title	Target Skill
21	A fun day with Sam and his Cat	CVC, Short vowels sound
22	Ben's pet hen	CVC, Short vowels sound
23	The vet and the fox	CVC, Short vowels sound
24	Max's day	CVC, Short vowels sound
25	The big box	CVC, Short vowels sound
26	Tom loves his dog	CVC, Short vowels sound
28	Shad the chef	Digraphs: sh and ch
29	Ben's Big Catch	Digraphs: sh and ch
30	Tim's day	Digraph: th
31	Tom and Matt at the park	Digraph: th
32	A duck's bad luck	Digraph: ck
33	Tom and his dad	Digraph: wh
35	Blue flag and black clock	Blends: bl, cl, fl, gl, pl,sl

Page	Title	Target Skill
36	Fast and fun	Blends: bl, cl, fl, gl, pl,sl
38	Brad and Fred	Blends: br, cr, dr, fr, gr, pr, tr
39	Greta's drum	Blends: br, cr, dr, fr, gr, pr, tr
41	Snack time with Smit	Blends: sk, sl, sm, sn, sp, st
42	Smart kid, new sled	Blends: sk, sl, sm, sn, sp, st
44	Ling sings	Ang, ing, ong, ung
45	The king of ping pong	Ang, ing, ong, ung
46	The king and his son	Ang, ing, ong, ung
48	Hank's gas tank	Ank, ink, onk, unk
49	Hank's junk	Ank, ink, onk, unk
51	The lucky rat	Reading practice
52	Kim at school	Reading practice
53	Greg and his dad at the zoo	Reading practice
54	Thank you	-

YOUR FREE GIFTS

As a way of saying thanks for your purchase, I would like to offer you a **FREE** complimentary resource **"Ben's Farm": an illustrated, decodable short story featuring simple phonics and CVC words for early readers.**

To get instant access just go to: **ecomclasse.com/free-gift**

- ❑ In this short story, early and struggling readers can join Ben on his exciting farm adventure, and learn new phonics and CVC words.

- ❑ With charming illustrations and decodable text, this story makes reading fun and engaging.

Introduction

Dear Parents and Educators,

As you know, reading is an essential skill that every child must acquire. However, for many young readers, learning to read can be a challenge. That's why instruction in phonics is crucial, as it provides the foundation for reading success. **Decodable texts** are a powerful tool that can help students of all abilities develop their phonics skills, unlocking the joy of reading and opening up new worlds of knowledge.

Our **"Decodable Readers" series** offers young readers a wealth of benefits:

❖ They can begin reading independently after learning just a few letters and their sounds.

❖ They'll be able to tackle unfamiliar words with confidence, using their newfound phonics skills to decode words accurately and avoid bad reading habits.

❖ By applying their phonics skills in the context of engaging stories and nonfiction texts, they'll experience the thrill of success and develop a love of reading that will last a lifetime.

❖ Encourage students to take turns teaching each other how to read a book by demonstrating how to follow words, lines, and pages: students can learn to follow words from left to right, read lines of text from top to bottom, and turn pages from left to right.

Our materials provide targeted practice that helps students solidify their decoding skills, building the confidence and competence needed to tackle increasingly complex texts.

Inspired by the **Orton-Gillingham Approach**, our **"Decodable Readers" series** is specifically designed to help early and struggling readers. By using our materials, students can practice and develop their decoding skills, becoming better readers of increasingly complex texts.

"Decodable Readers" series are organized into different levels, each book with a specific focus on foundational reading skills:

Levels	Target Skills
Level 1	✓ Short vowels ✓ CVC words (Consonant+ Vowel+ Consonant) ✓ Consonant digraphs ✓ Simple blends, initial position ✓ Welded sounds.
Level 2	✓ Blends ✓ Long vowels and vowel teams ✓ Consonants combinations and double consonants ✓ Magic e ✓ VCe (Vowel+ Consonant +e).
Level 3	✓ Open syllables ✓ Suffixes (-s, -es, -ing, -er, -full...) ✓ "ay" and "ed" sounds ✓ Twin consonant and non-twin consonant syllable division ✓ Vowel diphthong "ou".
Level 4	✓ Vowel digraphs ✓ "Consonant-le" syllables ✓ r-controlled vowels ✓ Trigraphs ✓ Silent letters "kn".

The focus of this book of the "Decodable Readers" series is to provide targeted practice in the essential <u>level 1 </u>reading skills.

"What Makes a Book "Decodable"?

Decodable books are often mistaken for easy-to-read books by non-educators. However, the term "decodable" refers to books that contain words with phonic elements that a child has already learned. For instance, if a child has already learned all the consonants and the short vowel sound of the letter "e," they can be expected to read words such as "pen," "net," and "Ben." Most decodable books also introduce some sight words, which may be phonically irregular or may become decodable once the child has learned additional phonic elements. As the child learns more phonic elements and sight words, they become a more skilled decoder.

Decodable texts must contain 70-80% words that are easy to decode plus high frequency sight words, allowing children to build their reading skills gradually.

In our series, we also introduce **high frequency sight words** that students are likely to encounter frequently in their reading, such as "the," "they," "have," "must," "love," "like," "a/an," "is/are," "some," "much," and more. By familiarizing students with these important words, we help them develop a strong foundation in reading and comprehension that will serve them well in the future.

Thank you for entrusting us with your child's education. We are committed to providing the best possible tools and resources to help them succeed in reading and beyond.

Unit 1

- ✓ **Short vowel sounds:**
  short a, short e, short i,
  short o, short u.
- ✓ **CVC words.**

Dan's fat cat

Dan has a cat.

The cat is fat.

Dan pats the cat.

Dan had a nap with the cat.

Liz and her big pig

Liz has a pig.

The pig is big.

Liz and his pig eat figs.

Ben and Meg

Ben has a red pen.

Ben lets Meg use his pen.

Meg draws a red hen.

Jon's dog

Jon has a dog.

The dog likes to jog.

They go for a jog.

My pup

The sun was up.

My pup had to run.

But the mud was too much.

Ann likes ants

Ann asks Ben for an ink pen.

She wants to draw an ant.

But Ben has an old ink pen.

Pam's cat

Pam sat on the mat.

Pam had a cat.

The cat is fat.

The cat sat on Pam's lap.

Pam had a hat.

The cat ran fast.

The red hen

Ben is a vet.

Ben has a red hen.

The hen likes to peck at the ground.

The hen lays eggs in her den.

Ben and the hen are good friends

My pig

My pig is big.

He likes to play in the sun.

The pig runs in the mud and has some fun.

Nat and his pup

Nat has a pet pup.

His pup is fun.

The pup can run and jump.

Nat takes him for a walk.

The pup licks Nat's hand.

Nat loves his pup.

A fun day with Sam and his cat

Sam has a big cat. The cat is fat. Sam likes to pat the cat. The cat likes that. Sam and the cat sit in the sun. They have fun. Then they have a nap.

Ben's pet hen

Ben had a pet hen. The hen was red. Ben fed the hen some wet bread. The hen laid an egg, and Ben said, "What a good hen!" Ben played with the hen and the egg. He let the hen rest and took the egg to his nest.

The vet and the fox

The vet had a fox. The fox was sick and couldn't run. The vet gave the fox some meds and soon he felt better.

Max's day

Max had a big cup. He filled it up with hot tea. Max sat on the rug and took his tea. His cat sat with him. Max felt happy.

The big box

The kids had a fun run in the sun. They ran and had lots of fun. They found a big box. Inside it, they found some dolls.

Tom loves his dog

Tom has a pet dog named Bob.

Bob likes to hop and jog.

One day, they went to the park and played with a ball.

Bob barked and ran after the ball.

Tom had fun playing with Bob.

They kept playing until it got dark.

Unit 2

✓ **Digraphs:**

Sh, ch, th, wh, ck

Shad the chef

Shad has a wish to be a chef.

He spends his time in the kitchen. He chops fish and adds some chips.

And then he puts it all in a dish.

Ben's Big Catch

Ben is on a ship and makes a wish.

He hopes to catch a big fish.

He drops his line and waits.

He feels a pull and says: "Gosh, it's a big fish!"

Tim's day

Tim did math and then had a bath.

He brushed his teeth and put on a thick cloth.

Tom and Matt at the park

Tom and his brother, Matt, are at the park.

They see a big dog.

"Wow, this dog is so big!" says Matt.

They play with the dog and have fun.

A duck's bad luck

Jack had a pet duck that was very sick. The duck had a bad luck. She got stuck in a truck. Jack gave her a big hug.

Tom and his dad

Tom is with his dad.

When Tom asked which tool to use.

His father said to whet the ax with the whetstone.

Unit 3

✓ **Consonant Blends:**

bl, cl, fl, gl, pl, sl

Blue flag and black clock

Bob has a blue flag.

He runs to see his friend Glen.

Glen has a black clock.

They play with the clock and flag.

Fast and fun

Clara has a slim sled.

Max has black gloves.

They go to the hill.

They slide down fast.

They play and have fun.

They are glad.

Unit 4

✓ **Consonant Blends:**

Br, cr, dr, fr, gr, pr, tr

Brad and Fred

Brad and Fred are friends.

Brad has a crab and Fred has a frog.

They sit on the grass and have fun.

Greta's drum

Greta had a green dress.

She played the drum.

"The music was great!" said Greg.

Unit 5

✓ **Consonant Blends:**
Sk, sl, sm, sn, sp, st

Snack time with Smit

Smit is a slim boy who loves to eat snacks. He took a snack and said, "Wow, this snack smells good!"

Smart kid, new sled

Max is a smart kid and got a great mark on his math test. He has good skills on math. He went to the shop with his dad, who wanted to surprise him with a new sled.

<u>Unit 6</u>

✓ **Welded sounds**

ang, ing, ong, ung

Ling sings

Ling strung her guitar's string and began to sing a song, but the strong wind stung her eyes and she had to stop.

The king of ping pong

Sam has a big thing for playing ping pong. He likes the sound of the ball. He is the king of ping pong.

The king and his son

The king and his son had a fun thing to do. They went to see the strong young men who could fling and swing long things. One man was very good at playing the gong, and he made it ring and sing all day long.

Unit 7

✓ **Welded sounds**

ank, ink, onk, unk

Hank's gas tank

Hank has a big tank of gas in his truck. The gas made the truck stink. Hank put on his pink gloves to remove the stinky gas.

Hank's junk

Hank had a big hunk of junk in his trunk, and he didn't know what to do with it. He called his friend Frank, who had a strong truck. Frank took the junk to the dump and got rid of it.

Unit 7

✓ **Reading practice: Mastering skills**

The lucky rat

A cat sat on a mat. She had a big hat. She liked to nap in the sun. But then she saw a rat! The rat ran and hid. The cat sat and waited. She waited and waited. But the rat did not come back. So the cat went back to her nap on the mat, wearing her big hat.

Kim at school

Kim is in class. She sits at her desk. The teacher is nice. She helps the kids learn. Today, they learn about bugs. Kim likes bugs. She thinks they are cool. After class, Kim goes to the playground. She runs and plays with her friends. Then the bell rings. It's time to go home. Kim likes school. She can't wait to go back tomorrow!

Greg and his dad at the zoo

Greg and his dad went to the zoo. They saw a big pig and a duck. Greg liked the pig. It had a baby, too! Greg said, "I want a pet pig!" But her dad said, "No, we can not take it home with us." They saw also a fox. Greg and her dad saw so much at the zoo. Greg said, "This was so much fun, I want to come back next Sunday, too!" and her dad said, "Sure, that's something we can do."

Thank you very much for choosing my book.

You had many options, but you chose this one and I am truly grateful.

THANK YOU for taking the time to read it all the way through.

Before you go, I would like to kindly ask for a small favor. **Would you please consider leaving a review on the platform? As an independent author, reviews are vital to help me continue creating the kind of books that make a difference for readers like you.**

Your feedback is valuable and means the world to me. Thank you again for your support, and I hope you enjoyed the book!

Leave a Review on Amazon US

Leave a Review on Amazon UK

Made in the USA
Las Vegas, NV
15 October 2024

96914858R10031